Siberian Forest Cats as Pets

Siberian cats and kittens

Includes health, breeders, rescue, re-homing and adoption, hypoallergenic traits, pictures and personality

The Complete Guide

By Alex Halton

Published by ROC Publishing 2013

Foreword

Siberian Cats, or Siberian Forest Cats, are one of three big-bodied, heavily-boned cats who are well loved for their status as goofy, gentle giants. Siberians, like the Maine Coon and the Norwegian Forest Cat, are seriously large cats. Some males will reach a size of 20 lbs (9.07 kg).

When a Siberian jumps on the bed at night, you'll know about it, not just from the way the mattress bounces, but from the rumbling purr that will emanate from the darkness around you.

Siberians are soft-voiced cats, more given to chirping than meowing, but they are also deeply affectionate and loyal companions.

Their intelligence and problem-solving ability make them wonderful family cats. Powerfully built hind legs allow Siberians to execute jumps their size would seem to believe.

To some extent, Siberians were a victim of the Cold War, long held close to home in their native Russia and only exported abroad in large numbers after 1990. In the past 23 years, their popularity has spread widely, and they are now one of the most beloved of all domestic cats.

A semi-longhaired breed with a thick, triple coat, they are amazingly easy to groom and have a very low concentration of the allergen Fel d 1. Although not truly hypoallergenic, they do elicit a much milder response in sensitive individuals. Whether this naturally occurring breed actually hails from the Siberian steppes or is simply a handsome product of Mother Russia is a matter of some debate. There is, however, no debate about the truly lovable qualities of these cats.

Foreword

Available in all colorations and patterns, including a blue-eyed, pointed variety, there is a Siberian for everyone. Once you have lived with one of these big, lovable beauties, you may well be spoiled for any other breed

Acknowledgements

Thank you to all my family and friends for bringing so
many beautiful felines into my life.

My obsession with Siberian Forest Cats has given me so
much joy – not only have they learnt how to tame, train and
touch my heart; they continue to treat me day after day.

Table of Contents

Table of Contents

Table of Contents

Table of Contents

Chapter 1 - Introduction to the Siberian Cat

The Siberian Cat, (also known as the Siberian Forest Cat), long a national treasure in Russia, only arrived in Europe and the United States in modern times around 1990. From the end of World War II until that time, their exportation was forbidden due to the hostilities between the Soviet Union and her Cold War adversaries.

Siberian Breed History

Figuring prominently in children's books and fairy tales in its native Russia, the Siberian Cat is widely regarded at home and abroad for its exceptional personality and unparalleled loyalty.

Legend holds that the cats were taken from Russia to Siberia where they stayed long enough to develop their distinctive, protective coats. Then, in theory, they were returned to Russia and bred primarily in Leningrad and Moscow. There is, however, no substantial proof of this claim.

In the 1980s, an interest developed in Russia for breeding pedigreed cats. The first breed standard for the Siberian Cat was developed by the Kotofei Cat Club in Moscow.

The International Cat Association (TICA) accepted Siberians imported to the U.S. in the 1990s into the New Breed program in 1992 and granted championship status to the Siberian in 1996.

While a practical working cat when it comes to rodent control, the Siberian Cat is also a magnificent companion animal. This is a naturally occurring breed, which is well suited to the harsh climate in which it originated.

Comparable Breeds to the Siberian

Often the Siberian is described as part of a "triangle" of similar, large-bodied "forest" cats. The other two are the Maine Coon and the Norwegian Forest Cat.

The real difference in these cats lies in the subtle conformation of their bodies that may not be apparent until you see them side-by-side.

Siberians are a study in rounded curves and circles, while Maine Coons are blocky cats have lots of rectangular lines. Norwegians, on the other hand, have a much more triangular appearance, especially in the face.

Physical Characteristics of the Siberian

On average, Siberians weigh 10-20 lbs (4.53-9.07 kg). Females are smaller than males. Classed as a medium to large breed, Siberians have a stocky build with especially strong hindquarters that make them powerful jumpers.

Overall, their bodies have a rounded conformation with few angles and good balance giving them a strong, capable, air. Their sweet and open expression is also alert and intelligent.

A Siberian's eyes will range from gold to an intense green. Blue eyes are a possibility in the Neva Masquerade colorpoint variety only. (Occasionally, two different colored eyes are also seen in this breed.)

The triple coat is thick, dense, and water repellent. The otherwise rounded ears are heavily covered in hair on the inside and slightly tipped. A ruff accents the neck, and the bushy tail, which is carried up is flanked by fluffy "britches."

All coat colors and combinations are possible, with or without white markings. Amazingly, the heavy fur needs only occasional brushing, and is not prone to developing mats and tangles.

A Siberian's coat does change seasonally, and the cat will shed in the spring in anticipation of the warmer months.

Siberians are slow to mature, and do not reach their full size until almost five years of age. Their projected lifespan is 11 to 15 years.

The Siberian Cat Personality

Siberians are adaptable cats. Regarded as something of a "gentle giant," these cats are affectionate, loyal, and love to be with their people.

Siberians are naturally calm and quiet, with an endearing, intuitive streak. They seem to know when the humans they love are in need of comfort and attention. When they speak, it's in a quiet series of melodic mews, chirps, and trills. Best of all, they purr loudly and often.

Motion of any kind will intrigue a Siberian. They play hard and have a daredevil streak, especially if you're on the other end of a "dangling" toy. This playfulness remains intact even into old age.

A problem solver by nature, the Siberian puts its keen intelligence to good use learning how to manipulate doors and latches, gaining access to the cat food no matter where you hide it, and deftly negotiating obstacles to reach its goals (generally without turning over or breaking a thing.)

Siberian Cats with Other Animals and Children

Like many cat breeds, Siberians have something of a tendency to pick a favorite person, but they are excellent family pets. They do quite well with other animals, including dogs, and get on nicely with young children.

In a single-person household, a Siberian will not enjoy being left alone for extended periods of time and may well need another animal friend, but this can vary by individual.

Children should be taught from a young age how to interact with all animals gently and with respect. Siberians exhibit good patience with children who treat them well, and will simply disappear if they don't like what's going on.

It is very rare for this breed to show aggression, but all animals will react negatively when they are afraid or they have been hurt. In the event of an incident, be realistic. Who really deserves to be "disciplined?" The cat or the child?

Hypoallergenic

Some Siberian cats have a lower than normal level of the protein Fel d 1, which is the primary feline allergen to which sensitive people display an adverse reaction.

Most breeds produce about 63,000 micrograms of Fel d 1, whereas Siberians put out about 1300.

All Siberians exhibit some level of Fel d 1, with the greatest concentrations found in those with silver fur. There appears to be no difference in Fel d 1 levels between male and female Siberians.

If you are interested in a Siberian for their low allergen qualities, ask the breeder if the kittens have been tested for Fel d 1 levels. This scan is usually done at 10 to 12 weeks of age. It is estimated that about 20% of Siberians will test very low for Fel d 1.

Chapter 2 - Locating and Working with a Breeder

Working with a high-quality breeder assures that you buy a healthy Siberian kitten. Beware of ads in the back of the newspaper, or worse yet, signs on street corners. These are the purview of backyard "breeders" who are, for the most part, running kitten mills.

Animals produced in overcrowded, caged conditions are bred for profit only with little regard to genetic integrity.

They are generally poorly socialized, and frequently suffer from a host of communicable and hereditary diseases.

This is not to say that there are not breeders who work from their homes. Their reasons are very different. They recognize that the work they do requires a 24-hour a day, seven-day a week commitment to the cats they are raising.

Many go so far as to add on rooms or whole buildings to accommodate the needs of their Siberians. You will not find catteries of this kind cranking out kittens as if they were running an assembly line. They don't offer their cats in pet stores, and if they advertise, it's only in cat specific magazines aimed at the cat fancy culture.

These are people who are absolutely passionate about their cats. They are the breeders with whom you want to be working.

(While it is optimal to buy from a breeder in your area, see Appendix II for a list of Siberian Cat breeders with an online presence.)

Also consider attending cat shows in your region and collecting business cards from exhibitors. Do not, however, try to talk to breeders about a purchase in the show environment. Cat shows are very chaotic, and exhibitors have little time to get from one event to the next.

The advantage of attending a cat show lies in being able to see examples of the breeder's cats and to collect contact information. Don't expect to walk out with a kitten.

What Good Breeders Require

Be prepared for the fact that you will have to meet certain qualifications to be considered as a viable candidate to adopt a Siberian. Adoptions are not "slam dunk" business deals. Breeders can and do refuse clients all the time.

Some of the things to which you will be asked to agree

(most in writing) include, but are not limited to:

- Neutering and spaying the cat before it has reached 6 months of age.

- Paying for a veterinary evaluation within 72 hours of adoption.
- Agreeing to the terms of a written sale agreement.

- Answering questions about your home and lifestyle.

Don't expect the breeder's involvement to end the day you take the cat home. Most will call periodically to check up on the animal. This is not, however, a heavy-handed business. Be sensitive to the fact that good breeders love their cats.

A breeder doesn't just want to know that you're treating the kitten well. Think of him or her as a benevolent grandparent who wants to see the baby pictures and hear all the cute stories.

Since your breeder is an invaluable source of helpful information, this is a friendly, productive relationship you will want to cultivate.

Questions to Ask the Breeder

As you're working with a breeder and learning about their cats, information needs to flow in both directions. Good breeders want to know about you and your home. They are concerned about the kind of life the kitten / cat will have with you.

You want a breeder who both asks and answers questions, not one who offers a lot of "canned" sales talk.

Think of what you are doing in terms of an adoption, because that's what it is. You are assuming responsibility for a living creature. The care of that creature is passing out of the hands of the breeder and into yours.

You want a breeder who is actively interested and concerned with the process, and you need to prepare yourself to be open to that.

It's a very good sign if the sales agreement requires that you provide proof that spaying and neutering have been performed on schedule, or that vaccinations and boosters are being administered.

You want someone who is just going to call up to find out how the kitten is doing, or who would like to see pictures. These are indications that you are working with a superior cattery.

By the same token, you will want to get straightforward, honest, and informative answers to a number of key questions.

- Are the kitten's parents healthy? Can the breeder provide certification of that fact, and better yet, can you meet the parents?

- What is the kitten's current vaccination record? What diseases has it been inoculated against, and what is the proposed schedule of boosters? What provisions will be made for the complete transfer of the kitten's medical records?

- Has the kitten been evaluated for any other conditions, including those that may be specifically associated with the given breed?

- Has the kitten been dewormed?

- Has there been a need for any other kind of veterinary care? If so, what are the details of that care?

- What are the specific forms of guarantee that are part of the adoption? What is included and excluded?

- Always ask for references for previous successful adoptions. If possible, it's a good idea to talk with people who have adopted kittens from the same cattery to get an idea of how the animals have worked out as family pets, and if there were any business-related issues with the breeder.

Always Ask About Socialization

Socialization is a very important aspect of preparing kittens born in catteries for their ultimate adoptions. Reputable catteries will not allow a kitten to be adopted before three months of age. At that time, the cat should be fully weaned from its mother's milk, totally litter box trained, comfortable using a scratching post, and well socialized.

Some indicators of thorough and successful socialization include, but are not limited to:

- Daily handling to accustom the kitten to human contact.
- The freedom to walk around and explore the nursery area.
- Interaction with grown cats after age 5-6 weeks.
- Interaction with kittens from other litters.
- Free access to a wide variety of toys.
- The free use of climbing and scratching posts.
- Exposure to activity in the environment.
- Exposure to well-mannered dogs and/or children.
- Exposure to a reasonable amount of noise.

Kittens that are raised in isolation of such factors will have problems integrating into new homes and will be subject to fear and anxiety. Siberians are not, by nature, a timid or reclusive breed, but kittens will still need to be properly socialized.

How to Recognize a Healthy Siberian Kitten

You always want to handle the kitten you are thinking of adopting, which is actually pretty hard not to do since Siberian babies are so adorable.

Beyond the irresistible cute factor, however, this will let you judge the kitten's muscle tone, and feel the texture of the coat, which should be clean and complete, without thinning or balding areas.

Very gently blow on the fur to make it part. This will let you look for any flaky or dry skin. Examine the areas behind the ears, under the "arms," and at the base of the tail for any flea "dirt." This is actually the excrement of the parasites. It looks like tiny flecks of black gravel.

A kitten having fleas is certainly not the end of the world. Catteries fight a constant war on fleas, especially in the warmer months.

The pests are persistent, and are easily carried inside on clothing and shoes. You do not, however, want to bring a kitten into your home with fleas. It can take up to three months to completely get rid of the little beggars!

Hold the kitten up and look into its eyes. They should be interested, curious, bright, and alert. Look for discharge in the corners of the eyes, and make sure there is none around the nose either. The baby should not be sneezing or "snuffling" as this can be a sign of an upper respiratory infection.

All kittens are a little timid at first, but they should be playing happily and completely relaxed in just a few minutes.

Take a kitten safe toy with you, or ask to borrow one from the breeder, and use it to see how the little one reacts. You should get a definite play response. Kittens are very adventuresome, and fancy themselves to be little tigers. They'd much rather pounce and play than cuddle.

(Don't bother with a toy that includes cat nip. Kittens don't display any reaction to the famous feline herb before 6-9 months of age, and some cats never develop a taste for "nip" at all.)

Expect A Lot of Paperwork

When you adopt through a cattery, you're going to have a lot of paperwork. This is also the sign of an excellent breeder, and not something to complain about.

The purchase agreement should stipulate the following details:

- Breed of the cat being adopted
- Color and pattern if applicable
- Gender
- Agreed upon price
- Names of the parents
- Full contact information for both the buyer and seller

Specific terms of sale may include, but are not limited to, some of the following provisions:

- Requirements for regular veterinary care including annual visits and vaccinations.

- Stipulations about grooming relative to the animal's coat type or other special needs.

- If the cat is returned to the breeder for any reason, there will be no refund (or partial refund depending on the reason), and certain medical tests will be required prior to acceptance.

(Usually the required tests are ringworm, FELV/FIV, and fecal parasite evaluations to be performed within the week of the return.)

Generally breeders require that their kittens not be given away or resold for any reason without their written consent. This is not only out of interest for the animal's welfare, but also to protect the integrity of the breeding program.

This prohibition is especially stringent in regard to shelters, humane societies, pet stores, and similar facilities. Breeders would far rather take a kitten back than to see it placed in any circumstance that would endanger its life or wellbeing.

Spay and Neuter Requirements for Adoption

Unless you are specifically buying an animal for show, most kittens made available by breeders are "pet quality."

They have some perceived "flaw" that disqualifies them from show or from breeding programs.

As part of the adoption agreement, they must be spayed or neutered.

Commonly the procedures must be performed before the animal has reached six months of age, and proof (usually a receipt from the vet) must be provided to verify that the alteration has been performed.

Declawing Expressly Forbidden

Expect your adoption papers to expressly forbid that the animal be declawed. This surgery has actually been outlawed in Europe, and in many parts of the United States.

Declawing is now widely regarded as an inhumane act of

mutilation. The surgery constitutes the amputation of the end of each of the cat's digits, and affects the cat's ability not just to defend itself, but also to walk and jump.

There are many effective ways to prevent a cat from destroying furnishings with its claws, beginning with early training to use scratching posts and extending through an appropriate program of claw clipping and maintenance.

This training should have been started in the cattery where the kitten was born, and it will be your responsibility to continue and to support these routines at home.

Guarantees Against Genetic and Health Issues

The breeder should offer a guarantee that at the time of sale, the kitten is in good health. Most contracts require the buyer to have the animal checked by a veterinarian within 72 hours of adoption to verify this fact, and to supply a receipt from the visit as proof of the verification.

Preparing Your Home for Your Siberian Kitten

Continuity is one of the most important principles to remember in transitioning a kitten from a cattery to your home. Cats, even very young ones, do not like change and will easily go "off" both their food and their litter box.

Find out exactly what the kitten has been eating, and what kind of bowls it's used to. Do the same thing for its litter box and litter preferences. Make everything the same to minimize disruption.

Cats have definite preferences when it comes to texture. This is true for both food and litter. Some cats like "chunky" others prefer "pate." Some want fine, soft sand, others think gravel is the way to go.

Especially until a cat is well established in its surroundings, it's best to honor those preferences.

Any future changes should be made gradually, with the full understanding that in the end the cat will probably win!

Make sure that all the toys you have on hand are kitten safe.

Pay particular attention to potential choking hazards. Remember that some toys, usually those involving string, feathers, bells, and similar augmentations are for "with supervision only" play.

Have everything you need to keep up with the kitten's routine, including grooming implements.

Getting a cat accustomed to being brushed and combed regularly from an early age greatly minimizes grooming needs over the cat's entire life.

Remember too that especially with a semi-longhaired breed like the Siberian, routine grooming helps to prevent or minimize hairballs.

Cat "Proofing" Your Home

Siberian Kittens may be small, but they have big ideas –
and little judgment. You have to take the correct steps to
protect the little darlings from themselves.

Curiosity truly can kill the cat. Be especially aware of
anything the cat can swallow or become tangled in and
perhaps pull something heavy off a shelf or table.

Invest in cord "minders" or tape electrical cords to the
baseboards. Cap open outlets. Products to accomplish these
precautions are easily obtainable as they are also an aspect
of "baby proofing."

Consider using baby latches on cabinet doors. Siberians are
extremely good at figuring out how to open things. Be
especially careful about areas where toxic household agents
are routinely kept.

 Never underestimate a Siberian's ability to get into
something. They are amazingly inventive!

Bringing the Kitten Home

Ask your breeder about the best steps to take in acclimating your kitten to its new surroundings. This is especially important if there are other cats in the household, or really animals of any kind.

Even with a fairly adaptable breed like the Siberian, it's a good idea to get the kitten established in an area that can be segregated for a few days. This will allow all parties concerned a little "breathing" room to get used to each other.

Often introductions with other pets are best handled through closed doors anyway. Cats rely heavily on their sense of smell, and can tell a great deal about one another by under-the-door sniffing and paw contact.
The first introductions face to face should be handled with supervision. It's important under those circumstances that you not overreact.

The animals involved will pick up on your tension. Just watch what's happening and let them sort it out for themselves unless a "rescue" is required.

Most Siberian kittens will be happily established in their new home within 7-10 days, including having worked out territorial and "pecking order" issues with other animals present.

Approximate Costs of Adopting and Keeping a Siberian Cat

For a "pet" quality Siberian kitten, expect to pay $750 (£495) to $950 (£630).
Show quality kittens cost $1300 (£860) to $1500 (£995) depending on the bloodlines involved.

In terms of monthly and annual costs, a Siberian cat is no more expensive than any semi-longhaired breed.

For a pet-quality Siberian, and assuming a lifespan of 10-15 years, the cost of keeping the cat will be $15,650 to $23,475 / £10,280 to £15,420.

That breaks down to $1,565 / £1,028 a year, or $130 / £85.40 a month.

(Note that with show cats that are being actively exhibited, other expenses will come into play like professional grooming, entry fees, travel, memberships, registrations, and so on.)

Adopting from Rescue Groups

Even with a cat as lovable as a Siberian, there are instances when an adult animal must be given up. These cats are in desperate need of a new "forever" home, and people who will take older cats are in high demand.

Since Siberians easily live to age 15 or more, you will still have an opportunity to have a long relationship with your new pet. This is an adaptable breed, and although it is never their preference to acquire a "new" human, a Siberian cat will handle transitions more effectively than many breeds.

If you do adopt a rescue cat, be aware of the following factors:

- Cats are highly territorial creatures. When they are introduced to a new home, they will be timid and anxious. Gently "confine" the cat to a small space first, perhaps a bedroom with an adjacent bathroom with everything they need — food, water, and litter box.

- Try not to overwhelm your Siberian cat. Let them get used to the sounds of the house, both inside and out. Interact quietly and lovingly with the Siberian during this period of time. Don't leave them alone, but make sure they have a small, manageable "safe zone" that he is in no way required to leave.

- When your Siberian does begin to venture out into the larger territory, let it look around, even snoop, without getting upset. You can establish boundaries later. Right now, the Siberian needs to understand where he is and get a sense for how he will inhabit his space. If there are other family members present, be sure they understand not to "fuss" at the cat.

- During this acclimation period, be especially sensitive about open doors or windows. When cats are scared they will often bolt first and think later. Don't give your rescue cat a chance to escape.

- If other pets are present, difficult as it may be, let the animals work out the pecking order. Siberians are gentle giants, but they're still giants. They're quite capable of defending themselves if they have to.

- Siberians are not aggressive cats, and generally when two strange felines meet the yowling and hissing is more "trash" talk than a serious altercation. The cats will likely be aloof at first, but they will come to an understanding.

- If you have a dog, allow the Siberian to assert his "authority" with a few hisses and swats. He won't hurt Fido. In fact, Siberians have a reputation for getting along well with dogs.

Most rescue cats adjust to their new surroundings in two weeks to a month. Just be patient and understand that for an older animal, this is a huge transition and not without a degree of trauma no matter how loving and gentle you are.

To learn more about rescue efforts with Siberians, see:

Siberian Cat Rescue Group (US)
http://siberiancatrescue.com/

The Siberian Cat Club (UK)
Rescue and Rehoming
http://www.siberian-cat-club.co.uk/view/14

Chapter 3 - Daily Care for a Siberian Cat

One of the most important things you can do for your Siberian cat on a daily basis is to interact. This is a very loving and extremely loyal breed. Siberians want to be with their humans, thriving on attention, affection, and play.

Of course, you must meet your cat's physical needs, but you have a responsibility to address the emotional requirements of your Siberian as well. Cats, especially Siberian cats, are not the detached loners they are made out to be.

A Siberian cat is a people cat. The first thing he wants and needs is you.

After that? Some nice service at the food bowl would be much appreciated for starters.
Nutrition Food and Water

All cats, regardless of their breed are carnivores. A dog can be fed a vegetarian diet and do just fine, but cats have a high need for protein.

Most breeders are in agreement that Siberians do best on a mixed diet of dry and wet food. Some catteries advocate feeding a "raw" diet, while others use high-quality commercial canned foods.

Some types of cats should not be allowed to free feed (have access to food left in the bowl throughout the day), but this is not the case with the Siberian cat.

It's perfectly acceptable to leave kibble out for your cat, especially in the first three years of life. Remember that your Siberian will not reach full maturity until age five, at which time it's best to cut back a little on the dry food to avoid weight gain.

Selecting a High-Quality Food

Discuss the matter of food selection with both your breeder and your vet. Always go with the highest quality food you can afford.

The general rule of thumb with commercial pet foods is the cheaper the price, the greater the amount of plant fillers the food will contain.

Cats need twice as much protein per pound as humans, and they need fats. They don't need plant-based carbohydrates.

The Raw Diet

{Note: The following is provided for informational purposes only and does not constitute an endorsement of the raw diet. Because the raw diet is used by many reputable Siberian breeders, the material is being offered in the interest of a complete, well-rounded consideration of daily Siberian care. Always discuss feeding programs with

both your breeder and your vet before dramatically altering your cat's diet}

The raw diet for both dogs and cats remains controversial. Many veterinarians are strictly against the practice, but those who are interested in holistic health care approaches are beginning to see merit in this eating program.

The theory behind this method of feeding is to give the animal the kind of raw foodstuffs it would eat if it were living in its wild, natural state. For an obligate carnivore like a cat, the raw diet consists of anything that could be obtained from a whole, fresh carcass.

Veterinarian Concerns with the Raw Diet

The potential danger of a cat contracting salmonella poisoning from raw food is an often cited as a concern by veterinary professionals.

While it is true that felines can get salmonella, it's important to remember that because their intestinal tract is short, cats have strong bacteria in their stomachs that allow them to digest foods we would never be able to eat.

With meticulous handling of the food itself, thorough hand washing, and the purchase of fresh products (mainly fresh poultry well within its expiration date) salmonella should not be an issue.

The best rule of thumb is to never feed your cat anything you wouldn't eat yourself. (That being said there are many human foods that are toxic to cats, a subject we will touch

on shortly.)

Vets also express concern about nutritional balance, pointing out, quite rightly, that commercial cat foods have known and regulated amounts of specific vitamins and minerals.

If you do decide to feed your Siberian a raw diet, it is imperative that you understand what nutrients your pet requires and take the necessary steps to make sure they are met.

Important Considerations with Raw Food

(No)

- Serve only raw chicken and beef, never pork or fish.

- Never keep raw food in the refrigerator past 2-3 days.

- Do not microwave raw cat food. Let it to sit out for a short period until it reaches room temperature.

- Keep your preparation space and all implements and receptacles scrupulously clean.

- Purchase a good quality grinder capable of adequately handling small bones.

Do Your Research Before Changing Your Cat's Diet

Before you consider putting any domestic animal on a raw diet, research the topic fully. Because cats are carnivores, there is a degree of logic to feeding them what they would be eating if they were hunting and killing their own prey.

However -- and this is an important "however" -- *an incorrectly prepared raw diet can be deadly for your pet.* The raw principle includes feeding bones. This represents both a choking hazard and the potential for throat and stomach tears and punctures from splinters.

It cannot be stressed strongly enough that a raw diet must be prepared according to set recipes with the use of special equipment to safeguard the health of your cat.

Things to NEVER Feed Your Siberian cat

Cats are just as susceptible to developing poor eating habits as their humans. They can get a "sweet" tooth, and they can

38

be highly skilled panhandlers. Don't let this business get started!

Feeding your cat "people" food not only contributes to weight gain and an unhealthy diet, but it also raises the real danger of your inadvertently giving your beloved pet something that is harmless to you, but toxic to him.

- *Never give a cat any form of caffeine including coffee, and do not let him eat chocolate.*

The real culprits in these food items are the methylxanthines found in cacao seeds. The extract is used in chocolate, and in a variety of beverages including soda.

If your cat eats any of these items, a series of dangerous reactions can result. These may include: vomiting, diarrhea, excessive thirst, panting, irregular heart rate, seizures, tremors, and even death.

Other foods that contain some level of toxicity for cats include, but are not limited to: alcohol, avocado, grapes, raisins, yeast dough, eggs, onions, garlics, and chives.

Do not let the cat get into anything that contains the sweetener xylitol, which can lead to liver failure among other complications, and do not let the animal eat an excess of salty treats. This can create an increased danger of fatal dehydration.

(For more information on this topic see: "People Foods to Avoid Feeding Your Pets" at http://www.aspca.prg/pet-care/poison-control/people-foods.aspx)

Be Careful with the Milk

While it is certainly true that your Siberian cat may enjoy a dish of milk or cream, proceed with caution. Cats don't produce enough lactase (an enzyme) to break down milk in their digestive system, a deficiency responsible for diarrhea and uncomfortable gastrointestinal upset.

Many adult cats are actually lactose intolerant, and experience the same level of discomfort from the condition seen in humans.

Adult Siberian cats don't need milk, and they don't get any real nutritional benefit from consuming it. If your cat shows signs of stomach upset after drinking milk, don't feel as if you're taking away some beloved treat by not repeating the experiment.

"Treats" of any kind should make up less than 10% of your cat's diet anyway, and you certainly don't want to give him something that will just cause a tummy ache or worse.

Water is an Essential Component of Nutrition

Provide clean, fresh water for your cat at all times, and change the bowl often. Cats won't drink from a dirty water bowl, and many prefer to drink moving water.

Consider the option of purchasing a water bowl with a re-circulating fountain. This will not only keep the water cleaner, but it will attract the cat's interest and encourage him to drink more.

Feline water fountains are not terribly expensive, retailing for roughly $30 (£23). Do be forewarned that Siberians are attracted by motion of any kind and may play in their water a bit. Having to mop up a few splashes is a small price to pay, however, for ensuring that your cat stays well hydrated.

Estimating Food Costs is Difficult

Obviously, given all the variables and all the options for attending to your Siberian cat's nutritional needs, prices can vary widely — especially if you opt to feed your cat a raw diet; then you will be purchasing and preparing beef and chicken.

As a preventive health measure, a well-rounded, high-quality diet is your pet's best defense against disease and the simple effects of aging.

The standard advice is to buy the highest quality food you can afford, in both wet and dry variations.

Plan on feeding your Siberian twice a day, morning and evening with some type of wet food, (about 5.5 ounces / 14.17 grams per serving), and free feeding kibble (.25 to .50 a cup U.S. / 0.208 to 0.416 cup UK per serving) throughout the day.

Conservatively, expect to spend about $50 (£33) per month on wet food and $25 (£17) on dry.

Depending on the style you choose, both food and water bowls should cost $5-$10 / £3-£7 each.

41

Litter and Litter Boxes

After food and water, one of your greatest responsibilities to your kitty is to provide a suitable and clean place to do the "business." Cats are fastidiously clean animals. If they go "off" their box, it's almost always for one of two reasons:

- They have an undiagnosed medical issue like a bladder infection and are experiencing pain getting in the box, which they are seeking to avoid by going somewhere else.

- They don't like the condition of their box and are looking for a more suitable place to eliminate.

- Cats are not all that fond of change anyway, and changes to their litter box environment can lead to disaster.

Litter Texture Matters to a Cat

When you bring your new Siberian kitten home, use whatever litter arrangement the baby has been used to at the cattery. Moving forward, your basic choices involve litter texture and box type.

Litters are available in:

- **Traditional gravel or clay.**
This is the least expensive option. As much as 10 lbs. (4.53 kg) can be purchased for around $2.50-$5.00 (£2-£4).

- **Fine clumping sand. (Available in single and multi-cat formulations.)**

Clumping litter is a good choice because many cats like the finer texture. (Be warned, if you have a vigorous digger, this stuff can fly.) NEVER flush clumping litter down the toilet unless the box specifically says the formulation is "flushable."

Many mainstream brands can be purchased in bulk. For instance: 42 lbs. (19 kg) $18 / £12

Designer brands that claim superior odor control with all natural ingredients are much more expensive, with as little as 1.4 lbs. (.63 kg) selling for $30 / £20

- **Environmentally friendly plant based materials like pine.**

These litters are also cost effective. For a pine litter, expect to pay about $10 / £7 for 20 lbs (9.07 kg). Some cat owners report good success with these litters if the cat becomes accustomed to them early on, but older cats who are used to gravel or sand will likely balk when they find their box full of shavings.

- **Absorbent crystals.**

Crystals are a relatively new type of litter that claim to absorb and trap urine and inhibit bacterial growth. Most are made of amorphous silica gel and are biodegradable. For 8 lbs. (3.6 kg) you'll pay approximately $16 / £11

Cats do have definite litter preferences. If you are going to attempt to transition your cat to a new type of litter, offer two boxes: one with the old litter, and one with what they are already used to OR mix the two litter types, gradually phasing out the old litter.

If you just present your Siberian cat with a box full of something completely new, don't be surprised if you get a ....surprise.

Box Type is Also an Important Preference

- A simple, open litter pan or box is the tried and true standard. These units can be purchased for $6-$10 / £4-£6.

The major disadvantage with open pans is that litter scattering is a major problem, and many cats do not like to be "watched."

- Covered boxes hide the unsightly evidence, and afford kitty more privacy. Depending on size, you'll pay $30-$50 / £20-£33.

- Automatic self-scooping boxes are popular with humans for many reasons, but can send kitty running.

Expect to pay $150 to $200 (£98-£130) for a unit of this type, but leave the original box accessible until you're certain your cat will use the mechanical one.

Training and Playtime

Siberians love to interact with their humans, and as a breed, they are so highly observant, they catch on very quickly. They learn language well, and are quite aware when their humans are pleased with them.

Some experts say that all a cat requires is patience from their humans. Anyone who has tried to convince a feline to do anything might be tempted to say the patience flows in the other direction!

Siberians, however, have a boundless store of patience for the people they love, and so are highly agreeable to notions of training – and they're always up for a game!

Leash Training

While the Siberian is not one of the cat breeds that will take readily to being walked on a leash, they are highly intelligent and trainable cats. The most important aspect of leash training is having the correct equipment, principally a leash designed specifically for a cat.

These units, which resemble open vests, put the attachment for the lead at the back of the harness between the cat's shoulder blades, not at the throat.

A popular model, the Premier's Gentle Leader Come with Me Kitty Harness and Bungee Leash is priced at approximately $11 / £7. The included leash has a "springy" feel, which diminishes the sense of resistance a cat can feel – and object to – on a conventional lead.

A variation on this theme is a harness design with a broader mesh piece across the chest. An example of this design is the Coastal Pet Pink Mesh Cat Harness, which sells for $12 / £8.

Some cats like this style because it feels more secure against their bodies and doesn't return a binding sensation along the straps due to the wider design.

You will likely have to try both styles to find out which your Siberian prefers. At first, just get the cat used to wearing the harness around the house without the lead attached.

Don't make any fuss about putting the unit on. If kitty objects one day, stop and try again on the next. It's imperative that there be no negative associations in the cat's mind with any part of this process.

Some owners report good success just leaving the harness and leash lying around near the cat's bed or on the sofa so their cat can look it over and give it the feline sniff test.

If a cat is reluctant about wearing the harness at first, don't try to buckle it, just drape it over their shoulders. At first, the Siberian will walk right out of the whole silly business, but in time, he'll begin to let the harness hang there.

That will allow you to proceed to buckling it loosely in place, gradually tightening the straps or to an appropriate fit over time.

A good rule of thumb is that you want to be able to run your finger under the straps, but the cat should not be able to wiggle out of the harness.

The first official "walk" should be indoors with the cat just dragging the leash behind him on the floor (and likely playing with it.) Don't be surprised if your cat plops down on his side and looks at you as if to say, "This thing weighs a ton!" Work with the Siberian in short 10-15 minute lessons until he pays no attention to the leash. Then and only then pick the lead up and follow the cat around.

That distinction is the primary difference between walking a dog and being walked *by* a cat. The leash is there so you have a way to prevent the cat from escaping and minimally controlling where he goes.

For the most part if you really want to initiate a course change, you'll have to pick the cat up. You'll be letting your Siberian explore the yard with you in tow, not the other way around.

With young cats, the process is much easier and shorter, but even older cats can be taught to walk on a leash. If an older cat has spent the majority of its time indoors, he will be nervous when he goes outside on his leash for the first time.

Stay close by and speak soothingly to your pet. In no time his native curiosity will have taken over and he'll think the whole business of harness and leash is the best idea *he's* ever had.

Teaching Your Cat Commands

Siberians have shown an excellent capacity to amass a working vocabulary and to respond to "commands." Any time you are attempting to teach your cat a "trick" or to elicit a desired response, cater to the cat's natural inclinations.

If, for instance, your cat is naturally given to using his paws, it's much easier to get him to touch an object in return for a treat and to increase the complexity of the behavior over time. Your Siberian will quickly catch on that a game is involved, and go along with you.

Limit any "lessons" to less than 15 minutes, and always reward your cat with treats as well as praise. Many people say that cats do not respond to verbal affirmations, but this isn't true of people cats like Siberians.

Siberian cats are pleased to please you and will try to be even more agreeable when their response garner lots of love and attention for their efforts. (Bear in mind that this

47

desire to please doesn't prevent a cat from completely ignoring you when you're unhappy with him.)

Cats can hear sounds at great distances. They can pinpoint the origin of a noise to within 3 inches (7.5 cm) of its exact location at a distance of one yard (91 cm) in under 6/100ths of a second.

You'll do much better getting your cat's attention by speaking softly rather than using the kind of "command voice" to which a dog would respond. Whispering gets your cat's attention far faster than "barking" at him.

A cat's hearing is roughly twice as good as ours. Humans hear in a range of 20-23 kHz, while cats pick up frequencies from 45-65 kHz.

One of the reasons cats often ignore men, especially those with deep voices, is that the speech may actually fall below the cat's normal "radar," which is pitched for high sounds, like the squeaking of a mouse.

Choose command words with clear, distinct syllables and try to pair verbal commands with visual cues. Cats communicate with one another via an elaborate system of body language.

You can tell a cat to get "down" off the counter, but he's more likely to learn the meaning of your emphatically downward pointing finger and read the displeasure in your expression.

Selecting Toys

As for toys, Siberians are excellent jumpers. Any toys that elicit chasing, running, and jumping, are perfect choices.

Dangling toys on wands that allow your Siberian to jump and swat and keep you out of harm's way of extended claws cost $8-$10 (£5-£7).

48

Remember that these are "with supervision only" toys. You need to be present and part of the game. Otherwise the string can be a choking hazard.

(Note that both string and Christmas tinsel also raise the potential for intestinal blockages if swallowed. These items can become twisted in the intestine and must be surgically removed. Be very, very careful in allowing your cat access to string.)

Beyond that, it's really just a matter of learning your cat's tastes. It's always good to have some toys that will stimulate your Siberian's interest whether you're around to join in or not.

One sure hit is some variation of a half closed ring or tube with a ball inside. Cats will try for hours to chase the ball and get it out of the enclosure. (They won't be successful; these units are very sturdy and therefore safe toys.)

As an example, the Petmate Crazy Circle Interactive Cat Toy (which comes in both large and small sizes) retails for $10-$12 / £6-£8.

"Crinkle" sacks and tunnels are also a huge hit because they not only provide a place to hide and watch, but also make a pleasing amount of racket when kitty goes rocketing through. (Note this is one toy you'll likely want to put up before bedtime so you can get some sleep!)

The SmartyKat CrackleChute Tunnel Cat Toy, which has a 9.5 inch / 24.13 cm opening and is 35 inches / 88.9 cm long retails for $10 / £6.

(Remember to never leave your Siberian alone with toys that have small detachable parts or lengths of string or ribbon. All represent choking or blockage hazards if swallowed.)

Opt For Larger Scratching "Trees"

You'll definitely want not just a scratching post, but an actually "tree" for these agile beauties. Putting a price range to scratching equipment is more difficult. The traditional carpeted pole will cost around $30 (£20).

Elaborate cat "trees" with perches, tunnels, and other hiding places can range anywhere from $100 (£65) to $300 (£197) and up.

If your Siberian does begin to attack the furniture, consider using herbal or adhesive scratching deterrents. Cats have an aversion to both pennyroyal or orange essence, which can be used to drive them off a favorite piece of furniture. You'll pay $12-$15 / £8-£10 for spray bottles of these mixtures.

Cats also dislike anything that feels tacky to their paws, which has led to the development of double-sided adhesive solutions to discourage scratching. These items retail for about $8-$10 / £5-$7.

Your Siberian's Grooming Needs

Even with their heavy triple coat, a Siberian Cat requires only minimal grooming. They are affected by the change in season, so you will see increased shedding in the spring, as the weather is getting warmer.

Otherwise, regular combing and brushing is all that's needed to stimulate the cat's skin, and to keep the coat healthy and clean. Select a wire-toothed comb that will reach down to the skin, but that will not pull at the hair.

A "pin cushion" brush (widely spaced individual bristles on a rubber base) is a better choice than a "slicker" brush. This kind of tool efficiently removes loose hair, and doesn't run the risk of damaging the cat's skin.

Pin cushion brushes retail for $7-$10 (£5-£7), and wire-toothed combs for $10-$12 (£7-£8).

Siberians are not prone to mat or tangle, but if that does become an issue for any reason, you will want to consult with a professional groomer or with your vet to safely shave away or remove the mats.

A cat's skin is extremely fragile. DO NOT attempt to cut mats out on your own. You can seriously injure your pet.

Chapter 4 - Siberian Cat Health

Overall, Siberian Cats are a reasonably healthy breed, but like all cats, they need your vigilant attention to provide the preventive care they can't give themselves. An attentive owner is the best health "insurance" any cat can have.

Spaying and Neutering

The vast majority of purebred Siberian cats that are sold by catteries are "pet quality." This means that, in relation to the accepted breed standard, the cat has some minor perceived flaw that prevents it from either being shown or used in a breeding program.

Such "flaws" are all but invisible to the thrilled new owner who is delighted to welcome a personable, devoted Siberian into their life.

However, spaying and neutering will be required as a condition of the adoption, since breeders are constantly attempting to improve the quality of their bloodlines and of the breed as a whole

Typically, the agreement stipulates that spaying and neutering must occur before the cat reaches six months of age, and that proof be forwarded to the cattery that the procedure has been performed.

Working with your veterinarian, there should be no problem meeting this requirement, since medically, this is the optimal timeframe for the surgeries to occur.

Although costs will always vary by specific clinic, there are inexpensive options for these surgeries in the range of $50 (£30).

Since spaying and neutering are the first medical procedures your cat will require apart from vaccinations, however, this is a good time to consider establishing a long-term relationship with a veterinarian.

Establishing a Relationship with a Veterinarian

With the high cost of just about everything today, everyone is in the position of attempting to save money. Having just paid for a purebred cat, many people have some degree of "sticker shock" and have an impulse to try to minimize the expense of spaying or neutering. That may not be the best option, however.

Most cat owners prefer to work with one veterinarian over the course of a cat's life if at all possible. This not only allows all the animal's records to be amassed in one location by one medical professional, but it creates a situation where your vet will know and completely understand your cat's health.

Spending a little more in the beginning to work with a vet in whom you can invest your long-term confidence is money well spent.

Program of Vaccinations

Vaccinations have been instrumental over the last two decades in dramatically reducing contagious disease transmission in companion animals.

At the same time, however, there has been some controversy about the potential for tumors arising at the site of the injections.

If this is an area of concern for you, discuss the vaccination process with your veterinarian so that you fully understand the purpose of each injection.

At the time you adopt your Siberian kitten, you will be given a record of any shots the baby has already received, and an indication of when the next "boosters" are to be given.

A normal program of vaccinations includes:

- Distemper combo

This shot is first administered at 6 weeks of age, with repeat vaccinations on a 3-4 week schedule until the kitten is 16 months old. A booster is then given at one year of age, and others at three-year intervals for the remainder of your Siberian cat's life.

The disease against which this "combo" provides defense are: panleukopenia (FPV or feline infectious enteritis), rhinotracheitis (FVR, an upper respiratory / pulmonary infection), and calicivirus (causes respiratory infections).

The vaccine may also include protection against chlamydophilia, which causes conjunctivitis.

- Feline leukemia

This injection is given at 2 months of age, and repeated 3 to 4 weeks later. At one year of age, your Siberian cat will receive a booster, with annual injections thereafter.

- Rabies

Rabies vaccinations are administered according to local law, typically on an annual basis with some type of legal proof of the inoculation provided to the pet owner. On average vaccinations are priced at around $40 (£26) per injection.

Practice Good Preventative Healthcare

Following a good program of preventive care that includes vigilant and loving monitoring of the animal's overall well-being is vital in ensuring the Siberian cat's long-term health.

Most people do not understand that cats have an approach to pain that is very different from our own. In their worldview, someone is always higher up on the food chain. To show pain is to open themselves to vulnerability to larger, stronger, more aggressive animals.

Consequently, cats hide their pain or ill health and can be very sick before their humans realize what is going on. It's important that you know and look for potential signs of bad health to spot a problem before it becomes serious or life threatening.

- Be aware of any changes in weight, either in terms of gains or losses. When a Siberian cat is at a healthy weight, you should be able to feel a pad of fat over the ribs, but still easily detect the bones underneath.

- Look for changes in how your Siberian cat moves and walks. Signs of a limp or of any reluctance to run or jump could be an indication of joint pain, muscle damage, or even an impinging growth under the surface.

- Watch for nasal dryness or discharge. A normal Siberian cat's nose is moist and clean, not dry, cracked, irritated, bleeding, or running.

- Discharge from the eyes is also a warning sign. Healthy Siberian cats have bright, interested, engaged eyes. The pupils should be perfectly centered, and the whites of the eyes should not be discolored. Also, there should be very few blood vessels evident in the whites.

- A Siberian cat's ears are prone to both irritation and parasitical infestation. Check for any sour or foul odor, and for any internal debris. The interior of the ear should be clean and smooth, not swollen and discolored. If your cat flinches when its ears are touched, a vet should examine the animal immediately.

- The gums should be pink and uniform in appearance, with clean, white teeth. Regular dental exams are a vital part of feline preventive medicine because they give the vet a chance to look for any lumps or lesions in the mouth. All cats are prone to oral cancers, which, if detected early, can be treated with a reasonable degree of success.

It's a good idea to start your Siberian cat on a program of dental care at a young age. It may sound insane, but most Siberian cats will be agreeable to having their teeth brushed.

Veterinarians carry oral hygiene kits, and will be glad to help you learn how to successfully work with your cat. The cost will be approximately $7-$10 (£4-£6) per kit.

Other preventive measures to take include:

- Monitoring your Siberian cat's breathing. Respirations should come more from the chest than the abdomen.

- Checking the body for any growths, masses, or bumps. (Always have these evaluated immediately)

- Watching for subtle changes in behavior. You will know your Siberian cat better than anyone. If you think something is not right, it probably isn't. Better to make a trip to the vet to be safe than to neglect a potential problem.

Watch for Changes in Litter Box Behavior

The number one cited reason for cats being given up to shelters is some form of inappropriate elimination.

If your cat misses, or goes outside the box, the first thing you must do is get the animal to the vet. Your cat may very well have an undiagnosed or chronic kidney or bladder infection.

In feline logic, if trying to go in the box hurts, they'll try to go somewhere else. They associate the box with the pain, and try to escape it.

Barring a health concern, your cat may not like its litter or litter box or, frankly, you may be the real problem.

Cats are very tidy creatures. If their box is not well-maintained and scooped daily, they won't want to use it. Would you want to use a disgusting bathroom?

This can also extend to replacing old boxes that have absorbed odors into the plastic of the pan.

Cats should receive a new box at least twice a year (quarterly is better). This will not only make kitty happy, but it will cut down on potential odors in your home.

Potential for Hypertrophic Cardiomyopathy

Like many purebred cats, there is a potential for Siberians to suffer from a thickening of the heart muscle known as hypertrophic cardiomyopathy (HCM), which is the most common heart disease among all felines.

In discussing health issues with your breeder, ask about HCM in their cattery's bloodline. Beware of a breeder who claims their line is completely HCM free.

There is no way to guarantee against a cat developing the condition, but most breeders will be prepared to discuss whether or not the problem has surfaced in their animals.

If a breeder dodges this question, be suspicious.

It is generally best not to buy a kitten unless the cat's parents have been specifically tested for the presence of HCM via an echocardiogram.

Sadly, HCM is a prominent cause of death in many companion cats. It eventually leads to fluid in the lungs, blood clots, and heart failure.

Feline Lower Urinary
Tract Disease (FLUTD)

There is now sufficient data to prove that Feline Lower Urinary Tract Disease (FLUTD) is a hereditary issue in Siberians.

This problem is inclusive of

urinary tract infections, blockages, and kidney stones in both males and females. (The risk of blockage from lower urinary crystals is higher and more dangerous in males.)

The condition can be successfully treated with special foods and a diet that emphasizes liquids. It is imperative that any sign of urinary problems be immediately investigated since left untreated, a blockage is not only extremely painful, but potentially fatal.

(Note that there is also some evidence to suggest that Siberians are prone to the development of benign cysts of the kidneys due to Polycystic Kidney Disease, once thought to be a health issue exclusive to the Persian Breed.)

- HCM – hypertrophic cardiomyopathy

- FLUTD – Feline Lower Urinary Tract Disease

- Benign cysts of Kidneys (Polycystic Kidney Disease)

Chapter 5 - Breeding and Showing Siberian Cats

Making the decision to become a Siberian cat breeder is not as simple as getting a pair of cats and letting nature take its course. While it might be just that easy for the cats, breeding is not just an idle hobby to be taken up lightly. It's a way of life, and one much more likely to empty your pockets than to make you rich.

While it is certainly true that purebred Siberian kittens command a handsome price, most breeders will quite frankly tell you that for them, a good year is one in which they break even.

Money goes out of a cattery at a much faster rate than it comes in. Simply multiply the expense of caring for one cat by however many animals you intend to keep and watch the dollar signs mount.

Weigh Your Decision Carefully

Never consider becoming a Siberian breeder until you have fully immersed yourself in the culture surrounding catteries and cat shows. You need to meet and talk with existing breeders, either in person, or online in discussion forums.

While you can certainly find Siberian specific discussion forums, any site that draws together a large number of cat breeders will be instrumental in helping you make your own decision.

All breeders, regardless of the cats with which they work, share the same kinds of problems. These people, who may well become your colleagues or competitors in the future, are an invaluable source of support and information.

Only people who are consumed by the same passion for felines that should underlie the decision to open a cattery can really help you make an informed decision.

Part of that process is a matter of addressing some difficult but crucial questions.

- Can you make the commitment?

This is not just a commitment of time and money, but also of space, dedication, responsibility, and even heartache. Your nights, weekends, and holidays may no longer belong to you. Part of your home may be taken over, or an addition may be required, to adequately house and care for your animals.

You will be working with living creatures that depend on you. Some kittens won't make it. Can you take that? And can you take giving up kittens for adoption, even to carefully vetted and perfect homes? How will your family react? Will you have support or constant opposition?

- Can you work out the logistics?

These logistics involve covering the initial costs of set up, acquiring a breeding queen or stud, housing multiple cats, and making everything work in a spatial sense. That extends to what the neighbors will think, and how they may react to increased traffic on your property. (Thankfully, Siberians are a quiet breed.)

- Do you have a back-up, failsafe plan?

Yes, as hard as it may be to contemplate failure in the beginning, this part of your plan is crucial. What happens to your cats if it doesn't work?

- Do you have a plan for placing your animals in the event that you start a cattery and then have to shut it down in mid-operation?

64

Remember, the welfare of your animals is paramount, which means always thinking about the worst case scenario while working to create the best outcome.

Work Out Estimated Costs

Be proactive about estimating your potential costs. Prices are dependent on individual circumstance, but make sure to include:

- Reference materials to understand the fine points of the Siberian breed and of its genetics.

- Your foundation animals. A breeding queen and/or stud or the applicable fees to pair your animals with those from another cattery.

- Repeat FIV/FELV tests for any animals that must go "visiting."

- Routine and emergency veterinary expenses including those associated with pregnancy. (Discuss all contingencies fully with the vet you will be using.)

- All additional cat furniture and toys including kittening pens and crates for transporting animals.

- Any construction costs including adding on to your home, or modifying your structure to keep intact animals separate to avoid unplanned litters of kittens.

Multiply your costs by the number of animals you will be keeping, and add on a reasonable amount for an emergency reserve.

Showing Siberian Cats

Generally, people who breed Siberian cats are also the ones who show them. Breeders are, after all, hardcore enthusiasts.

Cat shows allow them to display their animals and the excellence of their bloodlines, and an impressive list of awards lends prestige to a cattery.

This is not to say that an individual who owns a beautiful Siberian may not want to show that cat, but most exhibitors are also breeders.

This is one of the reasons cats shows are such an excellent resource for people who are considering adopting a purebred cat. You won't walk out of a show with a kitten, but you can certainly walk out with a fistful of business cards.

For this reason alone, you may find yourself in the cat show environment as a spectator, and it's imperative that you understand how to behave yourself!

The Dos and Don'ts of Attending a Cat Show

Spectators at cat shows have to remember the cardinal rule. DON'T TOUCH!

That's hard to do when your among so many beautiful animals. Try to remember that this rule is not to penalize you, but to protect the cats.

Most cat diseases are highly communicable. If you pet a cat infected with a disease and touch another cat, you've just passed along the bacteria or virus.

If you are asked to pet a cat at a show, consider it a high compliment and don't blink when the exhibitor hands you a bottle of hand sanitizer. Use it, and then enjoy the rare chance to interact with the cat.

If someone yells, "Right of way," yield. Move. Get out of the way. Or get run over! Cat shows are amazingly hectic, crowded, and busy places. When exhibitors are called to the ring, they have to get there in a limited amount of time or face disqualification.

Understand that if you're talking to an exhibitor who gets called to the ring, they will likely turn on their heel, take their cats, and leave without so much as a word. They are trusting you to know the ropes and understand that they aren't being rude. They're in a hurry.

If you are near the show ring when judging starts, stop talking and LISTEN. You do not want to do anything to distract the exhibitor or worse yet the cat, and, because judge make comments on animals while they are examining them, you'll likely learn a great deal by paying close attention.

Finally, if you hear the dreaded alarm, "LOOSE CAT," your only response should be to FREEZE. You should never try to help. Be quiet, be still, and do nothing more than signal the location of the outlaw animal should you see it.

The Mechanics of Cat Shows in Action

Cat shows are different from dog shows in a number of ways. Cats are only removed from their cages while being judged, otherwise they're kept secured at all other times.

The atmosphere is very hectic, and almost festive, with exhibitors elaborately decorating their cages and the adjacent area. In spite of all the activity, however, the actual progress of the show can be agonizingly slow.

Cats are far less receptive to being judged, and many categorically do not like the show atmosphere. Dramatic escapes are a panicked hallmark of these events.

Also, unlike dog shows, there will be a class for household pets, which is often a prime attraction for young people to become interested in the cat fancy.

The actual evaluation of the animals is done according to published breed standards formulated by the official body sponsoring the show.

The more completely an animal conforms to the points of the breed standard, the higher its score and performance in the ring.

All governing bodies have slightly different rules for how shows are administered. Details are available on the homepage of the given official body.

Examples include:

- The International Cat Association
- Fédération Internationale Féline
- World Cat Federation
- Cat Fanciers Association
- Feline Federation Europe
- Australia Cat Federation
- American Association of Cat Enthusiasts
- American Cat Fanciers Association

(Note that the Siberian Cat is a recognized breed by each of these entities.)

Final Thoughts on Breeding and Showing Siberians

Always remember that the idea of breeding and/or showing Siberians may, in the end, prove more attractive and "doable" than the reality.

You can very happily have Siberians in your life without running a cattery or ever showing a cat in the ring.

The only valid reason to become a breeder is love of the breed and a desire to improve its genetics. Breeding is a hobby, but it's also a way of life. Don't take it on lightly.

As for showing cats, although many people enjoy the process, and cat shows enhance many lives, it's really not a natural environment for a cat.

Siberians are adaptable, and cope reasonably well with being shown, but for many breeds, the stresses far outweigh any potential benefits.

Before you make a decision to breed or to show Siberians, learn everything you can about the cats themselves, and about everything that is involved with either activity.

These are not simple decisions and they should not be made on the spur of the moment or without full consideration for your welfare, but especially for that of your cat or cats.

Chapter 5 - Breeding and Showing Siberian Cats

terword

Apart from its sheer physical beauty, the Siberian Cat is a study in unexpected "features" that, when combined, make it an ideal companion animal.

Although its heavy triple coat evolved to withstand the harsh winters of its native Russia, the Siberian is a semi-longhaired cat with minimal grooming needs.

Simple bushing and combing are sufficient to keep this cat's coat healthy and gleaming. It is not given to matting or tangling, and only sheds heavily in the spring.

As an added advantage, the breed produces less Fel d 1 allergen than other cats, making it well tolerated by people with a sensitivity to felines.

Blessed with a calm disposition, soft voice, and adaptable frame of mind, the Siberian is a pleasant, empathetic friend who seems to know when you've had a bad day.

He'll give you a gentle pat with this paw in sympathy if that's what you need, but he also has a sense of humor and the timing to go with it. Your Siberian may well go for the laugh if he thinks that's the better option.

Although a big cat, with large males reaching as much as 20 lbs. (9.07 kg), Siberians are much more athletic than many people realize. They have powerful hindquarters and are capable of impressive jumps.

Since they're also cats to the core, with all the curiosity and intelligence that entails, if a Siberian wants to investigate something, it will. That being said, they are not destructive cats, nor are they loud. A Siberian will comment on your life, but with a chirp, not a yowl.

Afterword

Widely exported from Russia since the end of the Cold War in the 1990s, the Siberian Cat has gained well deserved popularity for the gentle, lovable giant he is.

A perfect cat for families, or for singles with other pets, you'll never regret welcoming a Siberian in your life.

Frequently Asked Questions

What's a brief description of a Siberian Cat?

A Siberian cat is a semi-longhaired, naturally occurring breed native to Russia. They are large cats, strong and well muscled with an active, inquisitive, and friendly disposition. The breed is comparable to the Maine Coon and the Norwegian Forest Cat.

Is the Siberian Cat a really a "forest" Cat ?

Like many breeds, the exact origins of the Siberian Cat may never be really known. They are definitely native to Russia. They are a naturally occurring breed. They do have a long history.

Apart from that, all that is conclusively known about the Siberian Cat is that it did first come to popular attention on a wide scale when breeders in Russia rescued street cats in Moscow and St. Petersburg in order to refine and standardize the breed.

Does the Siberian Cat differ greatly from the Maine Coon and Norwegian Forest cat?

Yes, although it is possible to confuse these breeds on first glance, the Siberian has the rounded most curvaceous shape of the three breeds.

Maine Coons are square and angular, while the Norwegian Forest cat has triangular features. These differences become quite clear when the three cats are compared side by side.

Are there many myths about the Siberian Cat?

The dominant myth is that the Siberian Cat originated from crossing a domestic cat with the Far Eastern Forest Cat (*Feline Euptilura*). There is absolutely no evidence to support this claim and there is general agreement that the Siberian Cat is a naturally occurring breed.

What kind of personality is typical of a Siberian Cat?

Siberian Cats are very intelligent, remain playful throughout life, and have a charmingly adaptable and empathetic personality. They are very loyal, and make excellent companions.
Thanks to something of a sense of humor and a tendency to be active and more acrobatic than their size might suggest, there's nothing dull about having a Siberian in the house. They like a good nap as much as they next feline, but they're always up for an adventure as well, and they're very good at solving problems and figuring out puzzles — like cabinet latches and door handles.

Do Siberians get along well with children?

Yes, the Siberian is a very good breed to have with children. It is important that all children be taught how to appropriately handle kittens and cats, and it is the parents' responsibility to teach these lessons.

Siberians are very loving with children who treat them well, and will simply avoid rowdy children they do not like.

How does the Siberian handle cold weather?

Mother Russia equipped the Siberian well against the elements. These cats have a dense triple coat that is strongly waterproof. Do not, however, let your Siberian be outside unaccompanied during the cold months.

They are certainly not impervious to the cold, and the world is, sadly, a dangerous place for our companion animals.

If started at a young age, a Siberian will do reasonably well on a leash, but these should be indoor cats for their own safety and protection.

Do Siberians tend to be healthy cats?

When a Siberian Cat is adopted from a reputable cattery run by a responsible breeder, you should be bringing an extremely healthy cat into your life.

It is a good idea to ask the breeder if the parents and offspring have been scanned for the heart condition hypertrophic cardiomyopathy, which can occur in cats regardless of breed or gender. All cats should also be tested for FeLV and FIV.

What is the difference been a pet quality cat versus a show quality animal?

Cats that are exhibited at shows and used in breeding programs are considered to be exemplary specimens of the breed, conforming perfectly to the breed standards set by the various cat associations.

These standards speak to physical qualities of body conformation and color, but also address temperament and demeanor. In most breeds, a kitten's quality becomes apparent by 6 weeks of age.

Any animals that have a perceived "defect" are deemed pet quality and are made available for adoption with the stipulation that they be spayed or neutered. This is an effort on the part of the breeder to maintain the integrity of the bloodline he is cultivating.

What are the patterns and colors of the Siberian breed?

The most common coloration for a Siberian is brown tabby with white accents, but all colors and patterns are a possibility.

Siberian tabbies are usually "mackerels" with a classic or marbled (circular) pattern being present, but less common.

Other colors seen in this breed include, silver, dark gray (blue), red, gold, cream, white, and black.

Pattern variations other than tabby include tri-colored Torties and Torbies. Shaded and smoke patterns are also seen in Siberians.

Does the Siberian shed heavily, and are they difficult to groom?

As with any breed, if you start grooming a Siberian kitten early (at least by age 6 months) and keep up a weekly or bi-weekly routine, the cat will be completely used to the process.

With a friendly breed like the Siberian, the one-on-one time will be seen as a treat.

Even though the Siberian has a thick triple coat, they are not difficult to groom with a good quality pincushion brush and a wide, steel-toothed comb. The cats don't tend to mat or tangle, and only shed heavily in the spring when warmer weather is coming on.

Does it matter if I adopt a male or a female? Does one gender have a better personality than the other?

Any differences in personality from one cat to another are based on the individual, not on gender and are dependent on how the animal was socialized at the cattery and how it was raised.

Siberian kittens that have lots of human contact and become accustomed to activity, noise, and other animals make great pets and are confident, friendly cats.

How large are adult Siberian Cats?

When fully grown, Siberians will weigh 10-20 lbs. (4.53-9.07 kg). They are the second largest breed of domestic cat after the Maine Coon.

What is the best way to select a Siberian kitten?

Take your time to research catteries in your area and visit more than one. Know something about the breed going in, and don't make an impulse decision. Especially don't give in to the urge to adopt the "runt."

You want to select a healthy, happy, well-socialized kitten from a high-quality cattery that guards against inbreeding and any possible genetic health defects.
(See Chapter 2 - Locating and Working with a Breeder for more information.)

Is it wise to buy a Siberian kitten over the Internet?

The very best way to adopt a kitten of any breed is to visit the cattery in person so you can assess the quality of the operation and meet not only the kitten, but the parents. Due to distances, this may not be possible.

Certainly you can arrange to adopt a Siberian from a breeder online, but there is always the question of safe transport of the baby. The Internet is an invaluable resource for research, but if at all possible, work with a breeder in person.

Should I buy one or two Siberian kittens? Won't one get lonely?

Siberians do need companionship, and if you have the room and the wherewithal to buy two from the same litter, you will be amazed and the wonderful relationship the cats will maintain for a lifetime. Litter mates enjoy a special and highly unique bond.

However, if you have an older, well-established cat, the Siberian breed is so adaptable the two should get on quite well. If you are away from home for long periods of time, the Siberian may not be the right breed for you, and this is something you will want to consider.

Although not as given to separation anxiety as some breeds, Siberians do like to be with their people as much as possible.

Why is declawing looked upon as animal cruelty?

To be perfectly blunt, declawing is cruel and is forbidden in Europe and in many parts of the United States. The surgery amputates the last joint of the cat's paw.

It is painful and extreme solution to a problem that can be handled with good training and adequate scratching equipment. The cat will not only be rendered defenseless for life, but its mobility is also compromised.

What do Siberian Cats need to be happy?

These are intelligent, observant creatures that are interested in what goes on around them. They enjoy being talked to and played with daily.

All cats need good quality food and proper veterinary care, but it is a serious mistake to think of any cat — especially a Siberian — as an aloof loner.

Siberians are loving, loyal, and empathetic. They want and need your company and will thrive on love and attention.

Why are some people allergic to cats?

People who are allergic to cats actually have a sensitivity to the protein Fel d 1 found primarily in the cat's saliva and sebaceous glands. Reactions vary from mild to strong, with some people reacting most strongly to shed cat hair, and others experiencing the greatest discomfort when changing the animal's litter box.

What is Fel d 1?

Fel d 1 stands for "feline domesticus allergen number 1." It is a stable glycoprotein present primarily in the saliva and sebaceous glands of house cats.

What is the source of Fel d 1 in cats?

Although primarily present in a cat's salivary and sebaceous glands, Fel d 1 is also produced by the lachrymal perianal glands.

One of the principal means of dispersal is via saliva on the fur from grooming that becomes airborne or is transferred to items in the cat's surroundings.

A high amount of Fel d 1 is also present in the animal's litter box.

Is there a reason why Siberian Cats have a low level of Fel d 1?

Although low Fel d 1 levels in Siberian Cats is a proven reality, there is no clear explanation why this is the case. If you are interested in the breed for this reason, ask breeders if they test for Fel d 1 levels.

About 20% of Siberians have exceptional low levels and cause little if any reaction in people who are otherwise sensitive to cats.

Tests on kittens are harmless, and can be conducted at 10 to 12 weeks of age.

Is it correct to say that a Siberian is non-allergenic or hypoallergenic?

Not even hairless cat breeds are non-allergenic. The issue is not in the animal's fur, but in the presence of the Fel d 1 protein. "Hypo" means low, so in reference to a Siberian's affirmable low Fel d 1 levels, which translate to lesser allergic reactions in sensitive humans, "hypoallergenic" is the accurate term.

How are kittens tested to determine the level of Fel d 1 present in their system?

Both kittens and cats can be tested for Fel d 1 by sending a saliva or fur sample to a lab qualified to conduct the required allergen test. Both methods are completely painless and do not harm the animal in any way.

Will a mother cat with a low allergen level always produce kittens with low Fel d 1?

Pairing a male and female cat that each have tested for low levels of Fel d 1 is the best way to attempt to produce kittens with low allergen present in their systems, but it is not an absolutely guaranteed outcome.

On the other hand, two cats with high Fel d 1 levels will always produce kittens with high levels that cause allergic reactions in sensitive humans.

Why is the litter box a major source of Fel d 1?

Although Fel d 1 is primarily present in a cat's salivary and sebaceous glands, it is also excreted by the anal glands, making the litter box a natural area of contamination.

Keeping litter boxes as far removed from family areas as possible to minimize litter tracking and cut down on dust will help to control dispersal of the Fel d 1.

Relevant Websites

Breed Profile: The Siberian - The Cat Fancier's Association
http://www.cfainc.org/Breeds/BreedsSthruT/Siberian.aspx

The International Cat Association - Siberian
http://www.tica.org/public/breeds/sb/intro.php

Siberian - Iams Cat Breed Guide
http://www.iams.com/pet-health

Siberian Cat Information - VetStreet
http://www.vetstreet.com/cats/siberian

Fanciers Breeders Referral List - Siberian
http://www.breedlist.com/siberian-breeders.html

Siberian Research (health)
http://siberianresearch.com/Home.html

Do Hypoallergenic Cats Exist?
http://pets.webmd.com/cats/features/do-hypoallergenic-cats-exist

Choosing a Healthy Kitten
http://pets.webmd.com/cats/guide/choosing-healthy-kitten

10 Tips for Bringing a New Kitten Home
http://animal.discovery.com/pets/10-tips-for-bringing-a-new-kitten-home.htm

General Cat Care Tips: How to Care for a Cat
http://animal.discovery.com/pets/how-to-care-for-a-cat.htm

Healthy Cats Guide: Diet and Nutrition
http://pets.webmd.com/cats/guide/diet-nutrition

Choosing a Veterinarian
http://www.humanesociety.org/animals/resources/tips/choosing_a_veterinarian

Hypertrophic Cardiomyopathy in Cats
http://pets.webmd.com/cats/hypertrophic-cardiomyopathy-cats

Things You Should Know Before Becoming a Cat Breeder
http://www.cattery-index.com

About CFA Cat Shows
http://www.cfa.org/client/Shows/AboutCFAShows.aspx

Glossary

A

Ailurophile - A person who is fond of cats, whereas an ailurophobe is an individual who is fearful of or dislikes the animals.

Allergen - The main allergen in cats is a protein, Fel d 1, principally excreted by the salivary and sebaceous glands, but also found in the anal glands. In sensitive people, this is the agent responsible for triggering a negative allergic reaction.

Allergy - As the negative reaction relates to Fel d 1 sensitivity in given individuals when they are around a cat, the allergy typically manifests with watering and itching of the eyes, sneezing, and potential skin rashes.

Alter - An animal that has been "altered" has been surgically deprived of its ability to produce offspring via a spaying or neutering surgery.

B

Bloodline - In pedigreed animals, the bloodline is a verifiable chain of direct descent through animals chosen specifically for their genetic quality. Bloodlines constitute a major portion of a cattery's reputation for excellence.

Breed Standard - All cat societies that sponsor breed cat shows and register given breeds work from a set of optimum criteria developed for each accepted cat breed. This criteria, which is based on optimum standards for points of conformation and temperament, is used as the basis for rating the quality of given animals for breeding and show purposes.

Glossary

Breed - Cats that are linked by common ancestry and that have physical characteristics that breed true (passed reliably from one generation to the next) constitute a distinct breed or type of cat.

Breeder - A breeder is a cat enthusiast who has chosen to create a reproductive program of carefully selected dams and sires within a given cat breed for the purpose of producing like offspring for show and sale.

Breeding - The sexual pairing of male and female cats (known as sires and dams, or studs and queens) for the purpose of producing like offspring.

Breeding Program - A breeding program is a crafted plan of reproduction of a given cat breed built around mating pairs chosen for their genetic superiority. The purpose is to breed outstanding specimens of the breed for show and sale as well as to preserve the genetic purity and quality of the overall breed itself.

Breed True - This term refers to the genetic ability of two parents within a breed to mate and produce kittens like themselves that exhibit all the except physical and temperamental qualities of the breed as established by a given feline governing organization.
C

Caterwaul - A feline vocalization distinct for its discordant and protesting nature, which is high-pitched and shrill.

Cat Fancy - This term refers to all individuals and groups (clubs, associations, and governing bodies) united in a common enthusiasm for cats, either as domestic pets, or as show animals.

Many members of the "cat fancy" are also breeders, dedicated to the preservation of the quality and high standard of given breeds of cat.

Glossary

Cattery - A cattery is an established facility that exists for the purpose of housing cats, usually those of an individual breed cared for by an enthusiast interested in enhancing the genetic quality of the line for purposes of show and sale.

Certified Pedigree - A paper or series of papers that attest to the verifiable lineage of a cat for purposes of registering it as a purebred example of a given breed recognized by a registering cat association.

Coat - This term refers to the fur present on a cat, which is typically short, semi-longhaired, longhaired, or "hairless."

Crate - Small, specially constructed transportation containers used for the purpose of securely transporting companion animals (typically dogs and cats) from one location to the next or temporarily confining them for their own safety.
Crossbred - A cat is said to be crossbred when its parents are each of a different breed.

D

Dam - The female member of a set of breeding cats, also referred to as a "queen."

Declawing - A surgical procedure outlawed in Europe and in many parts of the United States. The final joints of the cat's paws are amputated to accomplish the removal of the animals claws. Now widely considered to be an outright act of animal cruelty.

Domesticated - Any animal that lives with and perhaps works for humans in a tame and cooperative manner is said to have been domesticated, as opposed to "wild" animals who live in nature and largely apart from any voluntary contact with human beings.

E

Exhibitor - At cat shows, the owners of purebred examples of a given breed who compete with one another to gain recognition for their animals and perhaps for their catteries.

F

Fel d 1 - A glycoprotein that is present primarily in the salivary and sebaceous glands of house cats, but also in the anal glands. It is the principle source of allergic reactions in sensitive humans.

Feline - There are 37 members of the family Felidae in the world. Of those, 30 are small cats, including house cats, and 7 are the world's "big" cats including tiger, lion, jaguar, leopard snow leopard, mountain lion, and cheetah.

Flehmening - This distinctive expression in cats is often taken as a sign of displeasure or as a grimace. In reality, when a cat opens its mouth while smelling something, the animal is allowing air to pass over its Jacobsen's Organ.

Located in the roof of the mouth at the front of the palate, these two openings give the cat a highly specialized sensory ability to "taste" what it smells.

G

Gene pool - Within a collective body of organisms, the gene pool refers to all the collective genetic information responsible for the outcome of reproduction within the group.

Genes - A DNA sequence located on a specific portion of a chromosome responsible for determining a given characteristics of an organism.

Genetic - Inherited tendencies, characteristics, conditions or traits present in an individual organism.

Genetics - The scientific study of heredity.

Genotype - The genetic makeup of an organism or a group of organisms.

Guard Hair - The outer layer of a cat's fur comprised of coarser, longer hairs overlaying a softer, more downy undercoat.

H

Heat - In female mammals the point of the estrus cycle signaling receptivity to being bred.

Hereditary - Diseases, traits, characteristics, or conditions genetically passed from parent to offspring.

Household Pet - A cat that is not pedigreed or purebred and that is not registered to be exhibited or shown in competition.

Note that most cat shows do include a special category for household pets, but these animals are presented with ribbons of recognition, not awards that accrue points toward championship status.

Housetraining - The instructional process which accustoms a companion cat to live cleanly in a home, defecating and urinating in a specially designated box filled with some variation of "litter," normally clay gravel or fine, clumping sand.

I

Immunization - A series of injections, also referred to as "shots" or "vaccinations" for the express purpose of conveying immunity against diseases to the recipient animal or human.

J

Jacobsen's Organ - A specialized scent organ present in the roof of a cat's mouth and identifiable by two small openings at the front of the palate. The organ allows a cat to "taste" a smell.

L

Litter - A collective term for a group of feline offspring. Generally 3-4 kittens in house cats, although as many as 6 to 10 are possible.

Litter Box - A specially designated pan or container filled with either clay gravel or clumping sand that is provided to an indoor cat for the purpose of urination or defecation.

N

Neuter - The surgical procedure whereby a male cat is castrated and rendered incapable of fathering offspring.

P

Papers - Verified certification provided by a recognized feline association illustrating a cat's pedigree as a member of a given breed and used to register the animal for showing or breeding purposes.

Pedigree - A written record that goes back three generations to establish a cat's credentials as a member of both a given breed and a specific bloodline. Often the source of prestige for catteries and their prize animals.

Pet Quality - Any cat whose physical characteristics do not conform to the accepted standards for the breed and is regarded as unsuitable to participate in shows or breeding programs.

Normally pet quality kittens are offered for adoption with the stipulation that they be spayed or neutered. This provision protects the quality of the cattery's bloodlines.

Q

Queen - The female member of a breeding pair of cats, also referred to as the dam.

R

Rabies - A highly infectious viral disease typically fatal to warm-blooded animals. The virus attacks the central nervous system and is transmitted by the bite of an infected animal.

Registered Cat - Any cat registered by a recognized cat association that can produce documentation of its pedigree or ancestry.

S

Scratching Post - A carpeted or similarly covered structure in any configuration that has been designed for the express purpose of allowing a cat to sharpen and clean its claws inside the house. Designed to protect household furniture from damage by directing the cat's natural urge to scratch.

Secondary Coat - On a cat, the underlying downy fur found beneath the coarser outer guard hairs.

Glossary

Show - An organized exhibition of cats by breed in which judges evaluate the animals according to accepted standards with awards conveyed accordingly.

Show Quality - Any cat that conforms at a high level to the accepted standard for its breed and is considered suitable to participate in cat shows and to be part of a breeding program.

Show Standard - Formulated by recognized cat associations, show standards set criteria by breed for exemplary animals in terms of physical conformation and temperament.

Sire - The male member of a breeding set of cats. Also referred to as the stud.
Spay - A surgical procedure to remove a female cat's ovaries and thus render her incapable of producing offspring.

Spray - A territorial marking behavior typically seen in male cats whereby the animal emits a stream of foul smelling urine.

Stud - An intact male cat used as part of a breeding program. Also referred to as the sire.

T

Tapetum Lucidum - The reflective interior portion of a cat's eye that aids in night vision and flashes when subjected to light. Responsible for the "laser eye" phenomenon in many flash photographs of cats.

V

Vaccine - A weakened or dead preparation of a bacterium, virus, or other pathogen created for the purpose of stimulating the production of antibodies when injected subcutaneously. Designed to create immunity against disease.

W

Whole - A cat of either gender that is sexually intact, and has not been neutered or spayed. Capable of producing offspring.

Appendix I - TICA Siberian Show Standard

HEAD - 40 points
Shape - 12
Ears - 5
Eyes - 5
Chin - 3
Muzzle - 10
Profile - 3
Neck - 2

BODY - 35 points
Torso - 10
Legs - 5
Feet - 3
Tail - 5
Boning - 6
Musculature - 6

COAT/COLOR - 15 points
Length - 5
Texture - 5
Pattern - 3
Color - 2

OTHER - 10 points
Balance - 5
Condition - 3
Temperament - 2

CATEGORY: Traditional and Pointed.

DIVISIONS: All.

COLORS: All.

PERMISSIBLE OUTCROSSES: None.

HEAD:

Shape: Modified wedge of medium/large size with rounded contours, in good proportion to the body. The head is broader at the top of the skull and narrows slightly to a full-rounded muzzle. The cheekbones are neither high set nor prominent.

Ears: Medium-large, rounded, and tilt slightly forward. The ears should be set as much on the sides of the head as on top. Ideal position is one to one and one half ear width apart.

The hair over the back of the ear is short and thin. From the middle of the ear, the furnishings become longer and cover the base of the ear. Lynx tipping allowable.

Eyes: Large, almost round, with the outer corner angled slightly towards the base of the ear. The eyes should be set more than one eye's width apart. There is no relationship between eye color and coat color/pattern.

Chin: The chin is well-rounded but not protruding, and is in line with the nose.

Muzzle: The muzzle is short in length, full and rounded. There is a slight muzzle curvature, but the transition between the side of the head and the muzzle is gentle and inconspicuous.

Profile: The top of the head is almost flat, with a slight nose curvature of a gentle slope from the forehead to the nose and a slight convex curvature before the tip when viewed in profile.

Neck: Rounded, substantial and well-muscled.

BODY:

Torso: The body is medium in length, and well-muscled with the back arched slightly higher than the shoulders, with a barrel-shaped, firm belly giving the sensation of solid weight (which appears with age).

Legs: Medium in length. The hind legs are slightly longer than the front, and should have substantial boning.

Feet: The feet are big and rounded, with toe tufts desirable.

Tail: The tail is medium in length, wide at the base, tapering slightly to a blunt tip. The tail should be somewhat shorter than the length of the body.

Boning: Substantial

Musculature: Substantial, powerful.

COAT/COLOR/PATTERN:

Length: This is a moderately long to longhaired cat with a triple coat. The hair on the shoulder blades and lower part of the chest being thick and slightly shorter.

There should be an abundant ruff setting off the head. There is a tight undercoat (in mature cats), thicker in cold weather. Allow for warm weather coats. The hair may thicken to curls on the belly and britches, but a wavy coat is not characteristic.

Texture: Varies coarse to soft, varying according to color.

Pattern: Clear patterns are desirable, but secondary to type.

Color: All traditional and pointed colors and combinations are accepted with or without white. White or off-white allowed on chin, breast and stomach of tabbies; white allowed in most areas. Strong colors are desirable, but secondary to type.

OTHER:

Balance: Well-proportioned.

Condition: Excellent health in good overall condition.

Temperament: Must be unchallenging.

GENERAL DESCRIPTION:

The Siberian is a medium-large cat with the overall appearance of excellent physical condition, strength and power, modified by a sweet facial expression. The general impression of the body is one of circles and roundness. Siberians are slow to mature, taking as long as 5 years to reach full maturity. Females are considerably smaller than males, and allowances should be made when comparing females and young cats to the standard. Size is secondary to type.

ALLOWANCES:

Because the Siberian is a slow maturing breed, coat and physical structure should be taken into consideration when judging kittens and young adults. Buttons, spots, and lockets.

PENALIZE: Straight profile, narrow muzzle, long tail, delicate boning, non-muscular, long body, almond shaped eyes, very long legs.

WITHHOLD ALL AWARDS (WW):

96

Evidence of illness, poor health, emaciation, visible tail fault. Temperament must be unchallenging; any sign of definite challenge shall disqualify.

The cat may exhibit fear, seek to flee, or generally complain aloud but may not threaten to harm. In accordance with Show Rules, ARTICLE SIXTEEN, the following shall be considered mandatory disqualifications: a cat that bites (216.9), a cat showing evidence of intent to deceive (216.10), adult whole male cats not having two descended testicles (216.11), cats with all or part of the tail missing , except as authorized by a Board approved standard (216.12.1), cats with more than five toes on each front foot and four toes on each back foot, unless proved the result of an injury or as authorized by a Board approved standard (216.12.2), visible or invisible tail faults if Board approved standard requires disqualification (216.12.4), crossed eyes if Board approved standard requires disqualification (216.12.5), total blindness (216.12.6), markedly smaller size, not in keeping with the breed (216.12.9), and depression of the sternum or unusually small diameter of the rib cage itself (216.12.11.1). See Show Rules, ARTICLE SIXTEEN for more comprehensive rules governing penalties and disqualifications.

(*Source*:
http://www.tica.org/members/publications/standards/sb.pdf)

Appendix II - FIFe Siberian Show Standard

(Fédération Internationale Féline)

General:

Size - medium to large, females mostly smaller than males

Head:

Shape - a little bit longer than broad, softly rounded, massive

Forehead - broad, just slightly rounded

Cheeks - cheekbones well developed

Nose - medium length, broad, in profile shows a slight indentation, but without stop

Chin - slanting slightly backwards, in profile creating a curve from the upper line of the nose

Ears:

Shape - medium size, well open at the base, tips are rounded with well-developed hairs on the inside and tufts

Placement - with good width between, tilting slightly forward

Eyes:

Shape/Placement - large, slightly oval shaped. A bit oblique, set widely apart

Colour - any colour is permitted, there is no relationship between eye and coat colour, clear eye colour is desirable

Body:

Structure - well boned and muscled, powerful neck, broad chest, body in proportion to create a rectangular appearance

Legs:

Legs - medium high, to form a rectangle with the body, strong

Paws - large, round, well tufted between toes

Tail:

Tail - of medium length, thick, rounded tip. Covered on all sides by dense hair with no hairs trailing down

Coat:

Structure - semi-long, well developed, very dense, undercoat not lying flat, overcoat water repellent, slightly hard to touch.

Summer coat is distinctly shorter than the winter coat. The winter coat shows a well-developed shirtfront, full frill and knickerbockers

Colour - all colours are acceptable except pointed patterns and the varieties chocolate, cinnamon, lilac, fawn. Any amount of white is permitted

Remarks:

Novice class only accepted for cats born in the former USSR. Any crossing with other breeds prohibited.

Faults:

General - too small or too finely built

Head - long and narrow, straight profile, too round head (Persian type)

Ears - too large or too high set

Eyes - round eyes

Legs - too long or too thin

Tail - too short tail

Coat - too fine or silky, lying flat, lack of coat (except in summer)

Scale of Points:

Total - 100

Head - general shape, shape of nose, chin - 25

Ears - size, shape, placement - 10

Eyes - shape and colour - 10

Body - shape, size, legs, shape of paws - 20

Tail - length and shape = 5

Coat - quality, texture, length - 20, color/pattern - 5

Condition - 5

(*Source*: http://www.nic.fi/~amantes/standard.html)

Appendix III - GCCF Siberian Standard of Point (UK)

GENERAL DESCRIPTION

The Siberian Cat is a medium to large semi-longhaired cat, solid with "heft" rather than rangy. The most important features are head type and coat quality.

The overall impression should be of a cat with substance and rounded contours. Larger animals are preferred, though females will be somewhat smaller than males, but overall type is the overriding factor.

The Siberian has a very distinctive weatherproof coat unique to the breed, and, as the breed originated as a natural outdoor cat in Russia, the overall appearance of the Siberian Cat should reflect this natural heritage.

The Siberian matures slowly. Full development of the cat can take four to five years. The cat should have an alert expression, be in good general condition and well presented.

A cat should not be penalised if apparently wrongly colour registered, as there are no points for colour.

Head: The head should be in good proportion to the body. It should form a short, broad wedge with rounded contours, with a slightly rounded muzzle and chin. The lower forehead should be slightly domed. The profile line should show a slight concave curve at the bridge with a nose of a harmonious length. The nose should be of uniform width when viewed from the front. The whisker pads should be moderately well developed and form a gentle, rounded line with the chin.

102

The muzzle should be broad and rounded. The chin should be slightly rounded, neither receding nor prominent when viewed in profile.

Cheekbones: The cheekbones are the determining factor in the head type of a Siberian. The direction of the cheekbone arch extends to the outer ear base. The cheekbones should be low set, very broad and connected by a gentle, rounded line to the whisker pads and chin, which produces the desired impression.

Ears: Ears of medium size, rounded at the tip, set wide apart, the width of an ear or more between the ears. A cat with higher ear set but a broad rounded head is to be preferred to a cat with wide set ears but a narrow head. Ears should be well furnished.

Eyes: Large, slightly oval shaped, but with a rounded lower line, set slightly oblique and wide apart. Any shade is allowed except that blue and odd eyed colours are allowed in white and van patterned Siberians and only blue allowed in Colourpointed Siberians. The colour should be clear and bright as an indication of good health.

Body: The body is rectangular in format but not too long. The cat should be medium to large, well-muscled and heavily built with a broad chest. The neck should be short and substantial.

Legs & Feet: The legs should be in proportion to the body, of medium length with substantial bone structure and strength. The legs should be felt to estimate bone structure.

Paws large, with toes carried close, rounded and with well-developed tufts. A medium sized female with balanced bone structure and proportions should be preferred to a giant male whose legs are too long.

Tail: It should be broad at the base, of proportionate length and slightly tapering towards the tip. It should reach the shoulder blade. The tail should be well furnished.

Coat: The texture and structure of the coat are important features of the breed. However, allowance should be made for kittens that may have softer fur, and for the seasonal moult.

The coat is of medium length, with a very dense undercoat that is soft, fine and somewhat "springy," covered by a coarser, more substantial topcoat. The fur over the shoulders is shorter.

The hair is firm to the touch and waterproof. The smoothly flowing guard hairs should cover the back, flanks and upper side of the tail.

The underside of the body and the breeches have only undercoat. The undercoat is shorter than the covering top coat, it should be dense and plentiful. It may be lighter in the summer but should still be present. One should feel the definite resilience of the dense undercoat when a hand is placed on the coat. A longer, plentiful ruff is preferred.

Coat Colour & Pattern: The Siberian is recognised in a wide variety of colours and patterns including colourpointed. Chocolate, Cinnamon, Caramel and the according dilute colours (Lilac, Fawn, and Apricot) are not accepted in any pattern combinations (solid, bi-colour, tri-colour, tabby or colourpointed.) Burmese or Tonkinese colour restriction are also not accepted.

Any amount of white is allowed, (i.e. white on paws, chest, belly, blaze, locket etc.) on all patterns and colours including the colourpointed variety.

The colourpointed variety can be called Neva Masquerade. Allowance should be made for belly spots and shading on colourpoints.

SCALE OF POINTS

Head: Including general shape and balance; profile; muzzle and chin - 15

Cheeks: Cheekbones are the determining factor in head type - 10

Eyes: - 5

Ears: - 5
Body: Including overall shape; size; substance; boning; legs; paws and tail length - 35

Coat: Including undercoat; topcoat; ruff; breeches and coat texture and quality - 25
Overall Condition: 5

Total: 100

Withhold Certificates or First Prizes in Kitten Open Classes for:

- Narrow, high cheekbones
- Slight or delicate build, with fine legs and/or oval paws
- Straight profile, definite stop or tapering nose
- Long, triangular or narrow, oval head*
- Tail not in proportion to the body
- Soft, silky or Persian type coat*
- Protruding, round or small eyes
- Any defect as listed in the preface to the SOP booklet

* - Judges to exercise their discretion with kittens in respect to these points.

(*Source:* http://www.siberian-cat-club.co.uk

Appendix IV - Siberian Cat Breeders

Canada

BolshoyDom (Ontario)
WhiteGoldBreeder.com

Ellinnet (Ontario)
Sibercats.homestead.com

Finland

Aq-Bars
aqbars.com

Fin Amante's Siberian Cats
saunalahti.fi/amantes/

France

La Chatterie d'Artannes
chatsiberien.net

Germany

Andokajas
andokajas.de

Arctic Shadows
arctic-shadows.de/

Cattery du Palais d'hiver
du-palais-d-hiver.de/

Neva Cat
nevacat.de

Sibirische Katzen "vom Ohlenberg"
 vom-ohlenberg.de

Silky Tigers
silky-tigers.de

Snowknight
snowknight.de

Ireland

Forestside (Wexford)
nevamasquerade.webs.com

Japan

Almaz Siberians
homepage2.nifty.com/almaz-siberiancats

Netherlands

Cattery Hensha
hensha.nl/nl

Scotland

Chantaris (Glenrothes)
chantaris.co.uk

Dyfrig (Shotts)
dyfrigbirmans.co.uk

Sweden

Siberisk Katt
sibirikatt.com

United Kingdom

Lyndongraey (Godstone)
lyndongraey.co.uk

Lestvitsa (Southampton)
lestvitsa-cats.co.uk

Sayadaws (Southampton)
sayadaws.co.uk

Sibbycats (Bristol)
sibbycats.co.uk

Alchemist (Higham Ferrers)
alchemist.theleonardsmiths.co.uk

Nezhnaya (Chesterfield)
nezhnayasiberiancats.co.uk

Skyvalley (Hernel Hempstead)

skyvalley-birmans.co.uk/Skyvalley-Birmans/Home.html

Elmarlay (Kingswinford)
thecatsofelmarlay.co.uk

Mentobe (Oldbury)
mentobebirmans.com

Radzimierz (Churchover)
radzimierz.co.uk

Calder (Halifax)
caldersiberians.co.uk

Esaya (Thirsk)
esaya.co.uk

Luniktyen (Skelton)
luniktyen.com

Sapphirensteel (Choppington)
sapphirensteel.co.uk

Zool (Northallerton)
zoolsiberiancats.webs.com

Alexandrite (Crewe)
alexandrite-siberian-kittens.co.uk

Druzhina (Liverpool)
druzhina-siberian-cats.co.uk

Witchfyre (Preston)
cat-haus.co.uk

Snowtrees (Liverpool)
snowtrees.co.uk

United States

Prekrasne Siberian Cats (Arizona)
SibKittens.com

Lil Marvels (California)
LilMarvels.com

Siberian Beauty (California)
SiberianBeauty.us

Silversnow (Connecticut)
SilversnowSiberians.com

Majestic Oaks (Florida)
MajesticOaksSiberians.com

Cartier Siberians (Georgia)
Cartier-Siberian-Cats.com

Mystic Melody (Georgia)
SiberianCat.com

Shadowlawn (Georgia)
ShadowLawnCattery.com

Croshka (Georgia)
Siberian-Cat.net

Landmark (Georgia)
LandmarkRagdoll.com

Siberian Dynasty (Idaho)
SiberianDynasty.com

Sullivan (Idaho)
SullivanSiberians.com

TimberBend (Indiana)
TimberbendCats.com

Reigning Cats (Maryland)
ReigningCats.com

Kitails (Massachusetts)
Kitails.com

Siberkatz (Minnesota)
SiberKatz.com

Usta (New Jersey)
UstaSiberians.com

Sunbeam (New York)
BestSiberianCats.com
ForestWind (New York)
SweetSiberians.com

Nikarl, Nikkis (Ohio)   ?
Nikarl.com

Rozhenitsa (Oregon)
SiberianCats.me

KenMar (Pennsylvania)
YourLittleKitten.com

Inspurrations (Pennsylvania)
Inspurrations.com

Sibirskaja (Pennsylvania)
WillowSpringsPA.com

RocKaRan (Pennsylvania)
RockaranSiberKats.com

NevaMasKaRan (Pennsylvania)
NevaMasKaRan.com

KatyMcFurr (Tennessee)
KatyMcFurr.com

Astera Siberian Forest Cats (Texas)
RareSiberianCats.com

Pendraig (Texas)
Siberian-Cats.Pendraig.com

Vonleibchens (Texas)

Vonliebchens

Regal Siberian (Virginia)
RegalSiberian.com

Tormodkot (Washington State)
ForestKats.com

Glorious (Washington State)
GloriousSiberians.com

Russia

Charoit
charoitcat.com

Sibaris
sibaris.ru

Appendix V - Summary of Estimated Siberian Cat Costs

Pet Quality Siberian Kitten
$750 / £497 to $950 /£630

Show Quality Siberian Kitten
$1300 / £861 to $1500 / £977

Veterinary Expenses

Spaying and Neutering
$50 - $150 / £33 - £98

Vaccinations
$40 / £26 per shot

Routine Visits
$50-$75 / £33-£50

Basic Supplies

Food and water bowls
$5-$10 / £3-£7 each

Food
Conservatively, expect to spend $50 (£33) per month on wet food and $25 / £17 on dry.

Water
Feline water fountain $30 / £23 - Optional, but some cats prefer moving water.
Travel crate
$30-$50 / £20-£33

Litter

Traditional gravel or clay litters.
Mainstream brands - 10 lbs. (4.53 kg) $2.50-$5.00 / £2-£4

Clumping
Mainstream brands in bulk - 42 lbs. (19 kg) $18 / £12
Upscale brands - 1.4 lbs. (.63 kg) selling for $30 / £20

Plant-based materials like pine.
$10 / £7 for 20 lbs. (9.07 kg)

Absorbant crystals
8 lbs (3.6 kg) you'll pay approximately $16 / £11

Litter Boxes

Open pan or box
$6-$10 / £4-£6

Covered boxes
$30-$50 / £20-£33

Automatic self-scooping boxes
$150 to $200 / £98-£130

Grooming Implements

Pin cushion brushes
$7-$10 / £5-£7

Wire-toothed combs
$10-$12 / £7-£8

Scratching Posts and Deterrents

Carpeted scratching post
$30 / £20

Cat trees / playgrounds
$100 / £65 to $300/ £197 and up

Herbal scratching deterrents
$12-$15 / £8-£10

Adhesive scratching deterrents
$8-$10 / £5 -$7

Toys

As a discretionary expense, owners tend to get happily carried away in this category. Initially, budget $50-$100 / £33-£66

Projected Totals

Projected monthly
$130 / £85.40 a month
Projected annual
$1,565 / £1,028

Projected lifetime (10-15 years)
$15,650 to $23,475 / £10,369.74

Index

Made in the USA
Middletown, DE
29 August 2018